SEPTEMBER 2016

I0084466

Russia in a Reconnecting Eurasia

Foreign Economic and Security Interests

AUTHOR

Ivan Safranchuk

Eurasia from the Outside In

A REPORT OF THE
CSIS RUSSIA AND EURASIA PROGRAM

CSIS | CENTER FOR STRATEGIC & INTERNATIONAL STUDIES

ROWMAN & LITTLEFIELD
Lanham • Boulder • New York • London

About CSIS

For over 50 years, the Center for Strategic and International Studies (CSIS) has worked to develop solutions to the world's greatest policy challenges. Today, CSIS scholars are providing strategic insights and bipartisan policy solutions to help decisionmakers chart a course toward a better world.

CSIS is a nonprofit organization headquartered in Washington, D.C. The Center's 220 full-time staff and large network of affiliated scholars conduct research and analysis and develop policy initiatives that look into the future and anticipate change.

Founded at the height of the Cold War by David M. Abshire and Admiral Arleigh Burke, CSIS was dedicated to finding ways to sustain American prominence and prosperity as a force for good in the world. Since 1962, CSIS has become one of the world's preeminent international institutions focused on defense and security; regional stability; and transnational challenges ranging from energy and climate to global health and economic integration.

Thomas J. Pritzker was named chairman of the CSIS Board of Trustees in November 2015. Former U.S. deputy secretary of defense John J. Hamre has served as the Center's president and chief executive officer since 2000.

CSIS does not take specific policy positions; accordingly, all views expressed herein should be understood to be solely those of the author(s).

ISBN: 978-1-4422-5971-3 (pb); 978-1-4422-5972-0 (eBook)

Center for Strategic & International Studies
1616 Rhode Island Avenue, NW
Washington, DC 20036
202-887-0200 | www.csis.org

Rowman & Littlefield
4501 Forbes Boulevard
Lanham, MD 20706
301-459-3366 | www.rowman.com

Contents

Preface

In January 2014, the CSIS Russia and Eurasia Program launched its Eurasia Initiative. The vast Eurasian landmass, stretching from China in the east to Europe in the west and from the Arctic Ocean in the north to the Indian Ocean in the south, includes some of the world's most powerful and dynamic states, as well as some of the world's most intractable challenges. Scholars and analysts are accustomed to focusing separately on Eurasia's various regions—Europe, the former Soviet Union, East Asia, South Asia, and Southeast Asia—rather than on the interactions between them. The goal of this initiative is to focus on these interactions, while analyzing and understanding Eurasia in a comprehensive way.

Today, more than any time since the collapse of the Silk Road five centuries ago, understanding these individual regions is impossible without also understanding the connections between them. Over the past two decades, Eurasia has begun to slowly reconnect, with the emergence of new trade relationships and transit infrastructures, as well as the integration of Russia, China, and India into the global economy. Even as this reconnection is under way, the center of economic dynamism in Eurasia, and in the world as a whole, continues shifting to the East. The impact of these shifts is potentially enormous, but they remain poorly understood because of intellectual and bureaucratic stovepiping in government and the broader analytic community.

Following its twin report series on Central Asia and on the South Caucasus, respectively, the CSIS Russia and Eurasia Program is now releasing papers in a third series we are informally calling "Eurasia from the Outside In." If the first two Eurasia Initiative report series focused on how economic connectivity and shifting political alignments looked from the interior of Eurasia, the current series focuses on the perspectives of the large, powerful countries that make up the periphery of the Eurasian landmass, namely China, India, Iran, Russia, and Turkey, as well as the European Union. The six reports in this series, each written by a leading local scholar of Eurasia, seek to provide insight into where Eurasia fits among the foreign economic and security priorities of these major powers.

While the most visible components of Eurasia's reconnection are infrastructure projects, the longer-term result has been a reshuffling of relations between the post-Soviet states of Central Asia and the South Caucasus on the one hand, and the major regional powers on the other. When the states of Central Asia and the South Caucasus became independent 25 years ago, they were closely tied to Russia. Over the past two and a half decades, they have developed a complex web of linkages to the other Eurasian powers, who themselves have devoted increased resources and attention to Eurasia in the years since the Soviet collapse. Russia still remains the dominant security provider in Central Asia and most of the South Caucasus. However China, the European Union, India, Iran, and Turkey all play major, if still evolving, roles in the region as well.

The scholars we have commissioned to write these reports bring a deep knowledge of their respective countries as well as a strong understanding of developments across Eurasia. While they are addressing a common set of questions, their answers and perspectives often diverge. Our goal is not consensus. Rather, it is to provide the best possible analysis of the roles these states are playing in shaping Eurasia's reconnection. We chose to seek out scholars from the countries being studied so that these reports would not be U.S.-centric, but would rather throw light on how Ankara, Beijing, Brussels, Moscow, New Delhi, and Tehran conceive of their respective interests and strategies in Eurasia.

With this report series, and indeed with the Eurasia Initiative more generally, we hope to encourage analysts and policymakers to think about Eurasia in a holistic way. Eurasia is much more than just the periphery of the old Soviet Union: it is a patchwork of states and people whose relationships are shifting rapidly. It is Central Asia, but it is also Europe; the South Caucasus but also India. Most importantly, it is the connections that are emerging and developing between these various states and regions. Our "Eurasia from the Inside Out" report series highlights the extent to which the comparatively small states at Eurasia's center have become a focal point for the economic and political engagement of the much larger powers surrounding them, and hence why these states continue to matter for global peace and prosperity.

Acknowledgments

This report is made possible by the generous support of the Smith Richardson Foundation, the Carnegie Corporation of New York, the Ministry of Foreign Affairs of the Republic of Kazakhstan, and Carlos Bulgheroni. We are also extremely grateful for program support provided by the Carnegie Corporation of New York to the CSIS Russia and Eurasia Program.

The View from Moscow

Russia has always declared the countries of the former Soviet Union to be its top foreign policy priority. However, in the early 1990s few took this claim seriously. Russia's preoccupation with the West left less time and fewer resources available for pursuing an active policy in the Commonwealth of Independent States (CIS) space despite frequent declarations about the importance of this region. It was only during the first half of the 2000s that Russia started to conduct a more purposeful policy in the post-Soviet space.[1]

Russia and its leaders view the CIS as a region where Russia has vast economic, security, and political interests. Consequently, Moscow has tried to assert itself as a de facto leader of the region. Post-Soviet Russia has always viewed the European, South Caucasus, and Central Asian parts of the CIS space as an interconnected whole from the perspective of its economic and security policies, and has established and supported regional organizations that include member states from all three of these geographic areas.

Although more focused on the post-Soviet space, President Vladimir Putin sought good relations with the European Union (EU) in the early 2000s to facilitate economic growth and with the United States mainly on counterterrorism in the aftermath of the September 11, 2001, attacks. Over time though, Putin and his allies came to believe that the United States and the EU were seeking to extend their own influence in the CIS region at Russia's expense. In the last decade, to paraphrase Marx, a spectre has been haunting Eurasia—the spectre of geopolitical competition. The Ukraine crisis, beginning in 2013, is the most direct and damaging manifestation of that competition. The Ukrainian conflict has had a major impact on Russia's policy in Eurasia, and contributed to a newer "Turn to East" initiative that seeks to deepen connections between the post-Soviet region and the major powers of the Asia-Pacific region.

---

1. Russia's increased foreign policy activity could be sensed not only from the rhetoric, but also in budgeting. Russia's budget for foreign policy was volatile in the 2000s, but it noticeably grew right after Vladimir Putin became president in 2000. See Ivan Safranchuk, "An Audit of Russia's Foreign Policy," *Russia in Global Affairs*, no. 1 (2007), http://eng.globalaffairs.ru/number/n_7985.

Russia's Foreign Economic and Security Policy

While Russia's foreign economic and security policy has focused on the CIS ever since the Soviet collapse, Moscow has long recognized that the region faced threats from beyond CIS borders that, as the principal security provider for its post-Soviet neighbors, Russia would have to confront.

RUSSIA'S SECURITY POLICY

A number of issues constitute Russia's security agenda for Eurasia and the CIS space. Among other, these issues appeared as Russian priorities: counterterrorism and counter-extremism; averting Western influence and the fall of regimes through street protests or coups ("colored revolutions"); management of the so-called frozen conflicts in Transnistria, South Ossetia, Abkhazia, and Nagorno-Karabakh (with eastern Ukraine later added to the list); and deterring risks of spillover from Afghanistan.

Terrorism and Extremism

In the summers of 1999 and 2000, militants from the Islamic Movement of Uzbekistan (IMU) attacked government forces in southern Kyrgyzstan, presumably intending to cross the Kyrgyz part of the Ferghana Valley to enter Uzbekistan. The situation was so alarming that under the legal umbrella of the Collective Security Treaty (CST), signed in 1992, Russia and Kazakhstan assisted the Kyrgyz military and security forces. In the summer of 2000, militants from Chechnya attacked Russia's North Caucasus republic of Dagestan. Both the IMU and the Chechen militants had connections to the de facto ruling Taliban–al Qaeda coalition in Afghanistan.

In May 2000, Sergey Yasterzhembsky, Putin's aide, held a press briefing. He bluntly described the mounting security challenges from the Afghan territory, in particular al Qaeda's support to terrorists in Chechnya. Yasterzhembsky stated that Russia considered launching preventive strikes against Afghanistan.[1] Although this never happened, the statement made clear that Russia planned to react, and if possible preempt radicals not only inside CIS borders, but also beyond.

However, Russia lacked instruments for security operations outside of its own borders, much less beyond the CIS. The CST was functionally weak, and did not include all of Russia's post-Soviet neighbors. In the spring of 1999, Uzbekistan, Azerbaijan, and Georgia refused to extend their participation after the original treaty lapsed. Turkmenistan never signed the CST. In April 1999, Turkmenistan's president Saparmurat Niyazov requested that Russia withdraw the small number of Russian border guards remaining on Turkmen territory following a significant downsizing in 1994 and 1995.[2]

Even as the threat from Islamist militants grew worse around the turn of the twenty-first century, Turkmenistan, Uzbekistan, Azerbaijan, and Georgia stayed away from the CST and sought to strengthen their geopolitical independence from Moscow. Russia instead started to focus on deepening security cooperation among the remaining CST signatories (at the time these included Armenia, Belarus, Kazakhstan, Kyrgyzstan, Russia, and Tajikistan). In October 2000, Putin, in close cooperation with President Nursultan Nazarbayev of Kazakhstan, suggested strengthening the treaty, resulting in the establishment in 2002–2003 of the Collective Security Treaty Organization (CSTO).[3]

In 2001, the Shanghai Cooperation Organization (SCO) was established, which became another instrument for managing security in Central Asia. The SCO grew from efforts to demilitarize borders between China and the four neighboring ex-Soviet republics (Russia, Kazakhstan, Kyrgyzstan, and Tajikistan). This "Shanghai Five" developed into the SCO and included Uzbekistan as a cofounder.[4] The SCO pursued a wider agenda, combining security, economic, and humanitarian issues. Turkmenistan did not join the SCO, but kept contact with it, attending annual summits as a guest.

Within two years of coming to power, Putin oversaw the creation of the CSTO and SCO, which Russia has ever since regarded as key instruments for its security policy in Eurasia. Their membership and agenda overlap, leading to some duplication in activities and statements. Russia nonetheless prefers to keep both instruments, one with and the other without China as a member.

---

1. Юрий Чубченко и Александр Реутов, "Россия готова бомбить Афганистан," *Коммерсантъ*, May 23, 2000, http://www.kommersant.ru/doc/148558.

2. Niyazov simultaneously dismissed, and in 2002 arrested, the commander of the joint Russian-Turkmen border guard group, who was never seen again. See Иван Сафранчук, "Вызов для Туркменистана—афганская угроза," *Большая Игра: политика, бизнес, безопасность в Центральной Азии* 39, no. 6 (2014): 27–28.

3. CSTO was not set up from scratch. It combined disconnected elements that had come into existence between 1992 and 2001 under different conditions and for various purposes. The idea was to add common military command and political ground for regional units that were already in existence by 2002. They included the East European Allied Forces (Russia-Belarus military unit from 1999), the Caucasus Allied Forces (Russia-Armenia military unit from 1996), and the Collective Rapid Deployment Force for Central Asia (2001). Their convergence was legally formalized in the Protocol on the Formation and Functioning of the Forces and Facilities of the Collective Security System of Collective Security Treaty Signatory Countries, signed in Yerevan in 2001. See Ivan Safranchuk, "The Competition for Security Roles in Central Asia," *Russia in Global Affairs*, no. 1 (2008), http://eng.globalaffairs.ru/number/n_10358.

4. Despite its general aversion to post-Soviet multilateral cooperation, Tashkent even hosted an SCO counterterrorism unit (the Regional Anti-Terrorism Center).

While U.S. operations in Afghanistan after 2001 relieved some of the pressures Russia was facing from Islamist militants, Moscow increasingly came to worry about the effects of growing Western influence in the CIS space, which it took as a security challenge. Initial U.S. successes in Afghanistan appeared to give the Central Asian countries new opportunities, diminishing the attractiveness of Russia as a security provider.

United States, NATO, and "Colored Revolutions"

Resisting North Atlantic Treaty Organization (NATO) cooperation with CIS countries, not to mention NATO's expansion into the CIS space or the establishment of a foreign military presence in the post-Soviet region, has always been an important element of Russia's security agenda for Eurasia. In the 1990s, Western countries were defined (with regard to the CIS space) by Russian officials as "extraregional."

With Russia's growing assertiveness after 2000, Moscow was even more willing to take responsibility for Central Asia. However, under the pressure of terrorism-related risks at that time, Russia was open to cooperating with China (establishing the SCO in June 2001) and the United States (agreeing to a U.S. military presence in the region in October 2001). The United States soon based forces in Kyrgyzstan (Manas) and Uzbekistan (Karshi-Khanabad) to support the international coalition fighting in Afghanistan. For the same purpose Germany and France also established a military presence in Uzbekistan (Termez) and Tajikistan (Kulob, later Dushanbe), respectively.

Putin's approval of U.S. forces in Central Asia in no way altered Moscow's long-standing position of opposing a permanent foreign military presence within the CIS space. Russia accepted the stationing of U.S. (and French and German) forces in Central Asia as only Afghanistan-related and only on a temporary basis (for the initial stage of operations in Afghanistan). Putin's acceptance also came at a positive moment in Russian-U.S. relations, which had been improving after the June 2001 meeting between President Putin and President George W. Bush in Ljubljana, and even more after the 9/11 attacks. With conditions eroding by the mid-2000s, the presence of U.S. forces in Central Asia ultimately became a source of tension between Washington and Moscow, as Russian officials came to see the U.S. deployment as a threat to Russian influence. Moreover, Russia was coming to have similar concerns about the growth of U.S. influence in the South Caucasus and Eastern European parts of the CIS as well.

A few elements contributed to the erosion of Russia's support for the U.S. military presence. Russia viewed U.S. policy in the Middle East with suspicion. The possibility of the Bush administration invading Iran after Iraq could not be dismissed, a possibility that was a major concern to Russia, including in the context of Central Asia and South Caucasus regions.[5] Although some CIS countries participated in the U.S. mission in Iraq, Iran would have been far more controversial. Besides, Russia did not see reciprocal cooperation from the United States and NATO when it came to the CIS. NATO (generally perceived in Moscow as meaning the United States) continuously refused to engage with or recognize the CSTO as a counterpart. Moscow had sought a relationship on multiple occasions, including encouraging a NATO-CSTO deal on transit to Afghanistan.

---

5. Сергей Караганов, "О России, США и Центральной Азии," *Российская газета*, October 20, 2005, https://rg.ru/2005/10/20/asia.html.

Two other issues, however, appeared decisive: the possibility that the U.S. deployments in Central Asia would prove to be permanent, and the outbreak of "colored revolutions" in several CIS states. Thus, for Russia, "colored revolutions," a foreign military presence in the CIS, and NATO expansion looked like a snarled ball of security challenges, rolling through Russia's zone of influence.

Debates in Washington on changing military basing priorities and the then-popular idea of "lily pads" (small but expandable jumping-off points) around the world that U.S. forces could use in a crisis[6] were important concerns for Russia because the U.S. military presence in Central Asia might become long-lasting. Of course, Russia's own military presence in Eastern Europe, Central Asia, and the South Caucasus was far more robust, with several sites in Ukraine (Crimea), Kazakhstan, Kyrgyzstan, Tajikistan, Armenia, Azerbaijan, Georgia, Moldova (Transnistria), and Belarus. But in many of these countries, local authorities opposed further military cooperation with Russia, and pressured Moscow either to withdraw its forces or to substantially increase the rent it was paying for these facilities.[7]

By the middle of the 2000s, a perception that Russian power in the CIS was in retreat came to predominate. Even CSTO members were seeking greater cooperation with the United States and NATO. Those most inclined to cooperation with NATO and the United States countries stricken by "colored revolutions." These were Georgia (December 2003), Ukraine (November 2004), and CSTO member Kyrgyzstan (March 2005). In each case the new authorities called for closer cooperation with the United States and Europe; Ukraine and Georgia even aspired to NATO membership. Kyrgyzstan, though far from NATO territory, became increasingly cooperative with regard to the U.S. military presence under the leadership of President Kurmanbek Bakiyev.

The successful "colored revolutions" challenged Russia's influence in the region and contributed to Russia's perception of retreat. Russia reacted by getting tougher on the West in general. This step did not help Moscow win back influence with its post-Soviet neighbors. The fear of "colored revolutions" on the parts of the governments of Uzbekistan and Kazakhstan (the two biggest countries in the region), however, saved Russia's strategic position in Central Asia.

Uzbek-U.S. relations improved significantly from late 2001. President Islam Karimov allowed parts of his security apparatus to deeply cooperate with the United States.[8] At the same time, the United States dramatically increased economic assistance to Uzbekistan.[9] Already in 2004, though,

---

6. Kurt M. Campbell and Celeste Johnson Ward, "New Battle Stations?," *Foreign Affairs*, September/October 2003.

7. In 1999, Russia had to withdraw all its border guards from Turkmenistan. These forces had helped Russia to contain the spread of radicalism and other risks from Afghanistan. In 2005, Russian border guards were also forced to leave the Tajik-Afghan border. Russia still kept a military presence in Tajikistan, but overall military cooperation was shrinking. Georgia and Moldova demanded Russia withdraw all military bases from their territories, including those stationed in breakaway regions of South Ossetia, Abkhazia, and Transnistria, which were not under the de facto control of the governments in Tbilisi or Chişinău. The governments of Kazakhstan, Ukraine, and Azerbaijan pressed Russia for higher rent payments.

8. Seth G. Jones et al., *Securing Tyrants or Fostering Reform? U.S. Internal Security Assistance to Repressive and Transitioning Regimes* (Santa Monica, CA: RAND, 2006), 49–88, http://www.rand.org/content/dam/rand/pubs /monographs/2006/RAND_MG550.pdf.

9. From 2001 to 2005, Uzbekistan received $483.3 million in U.S. aid (double what it had received in 1992–2000). See Ольга Оликер, "Политика США в ЦА: реформы и безопасность," *Большая Игра: политика, бизнес, безопасность в Центральной Азии* 7, no. 1 (2008): 31–46.

relations started stumbling, with Uzbek authorities becoming less open and cooperative.[10] A dramatic worsening came in 2005.

In May 2005, Uzbekistan experienced an uprising by a coalition of Islamists and grassroot business and social networks in Andijon. Western media, nongovernmental organizations (NGOs), and expert commentators expressed overwhelming solidarity with the rebels, whom the Uzbek government treated as terrorists.

In response to calls by some U.S. officials for an international investigation, Tashkent demanded the withdrawal of the U.S. military from the Karshi-Khanabad base. The United States had to withdraw.[11] Additionally, Uzbek authorities cracked down on NGOs and civil society, which further spoiled relations with Western countries. The United States heavily criticized Tashkent, and the European Union imposed sanctions.

Kazakhstan was meanwhile experiencing its own problems with the United States. In 2003, James Giffen, a U.S. businessman and facilitator with close ties to the Kazakh government, was arrested in the United States on corruption charges, starting a case that came to be known in the United States as Kazakhgate. The arrest was perceived with extreme concern in Astana because a trial could bring into the open sensitive information about President Nursultan Nazarbayev's family and Kazakhstan's elite more broadly. Astana believed the arrest was designed to send some kind of message, one that the Kazakh government could not exactly understand, yet finally tending to take it as challenge to Nazarbayev's personal power. This coincided with growing internal pressure on Nazarbayev from within the Kazakh elite, including members of his own family. Thus, Nazarbayev's confidence in the United States declined dramatically through the 2000s. Only after the 2008 war conflict between Russia and Georgia did Astana and Washington again find some common ground.

The countries that had experienced "colored revolutions" and installed new pro-Western governments were also going through difficulties by the second half of the 2000s, breeding disenchantment with the United States and renewed interest in boosting ties with Russia. Only President Mikheil Saakashvili in Georgia proved able to pursue a number of reforms that substantially improved the economic situation. But even in Georgia, let alone in Ukraine and Kyrgyzstan, internal opposition was on the rise, with protests on many social and political issues, including the worsening of relations with Russia.

In 2006, a truck driven by an American killed a Kyrgyz worker at the Manas air base. The accident sparked a wave of protests, which in turn made the future of the base a prominent political issue in Kyrgyzstan, with internal opposition growing. President Bakiyev's position was ambiguous, as he was balancing relations with the United States and Russia.[12] In 2009, Russia provided Kyrgyzstan

---

10. Two events most likely contributed to this shift. First, in August 2003, on his way back home from the Organization of Islamic Cooperation summit in Malaysia, Putin landed briefly in Samarkand to meet President Karimov for what was supposedly a frank informal exchange of views. Second, Tashkent could not overlook the implications of the Rose Revolution that shook Georgia in December 2003 and resulted in the ouster of President Eduard Shevardnadze.

11. Some of the airpower was shifted to the Manas base in Bishkek.

12. President Bakiyev pushed the United States to increase rent payments for the base, either as an attempt to create a pretext to squeeze the base out (on economic reasons rather than pure political reasons), or in an attempt to maximize

with a multibillion dollar loan and, after negotiations in Moscow in April 2009, Bakiyev announced his decision to close the base. In the next month, the necessary legislation was passed and signed by the president. However, in June 2009, the decision was reversed, because the United States agreed to convert the base into an "international transit center," ostensibly making it more transparent for the local authorities, and substantially increased the annual rent payments.

The U.S. push to provide Ukraine and Georgia with membership action plans (MAPs) at the 2008 NATO summit in Bucharest faced intractable resistance from many leading European alliance members. Georgia and Ukraine were merely provided vague assurances that at some point in the future they would be NATO members. With the Bucharest declaration, NATO expansion stopped short of CIS frontiers.

By 2008, the security situation for Russia in the CIS region had improved in many ways. The wave of "colored revolutions" had been interrupted and seemed close to being reversed. A non-Russian military presence in the CIS also did not develop; U.S. forces withdrew from Uzbekistan and were under mounting pressure to leave Kyrgyzstan. Generally Russia, to its satisfaction, seemed to have made progress in solving the interlocking challenges posed by "colored revolutions" and NATO expansion.

India and China

Russia resisted not only Western, but rather all external military penetration into the post-Soviet region. From 2002, India invested in Tajikistan's Ayni air base, upgrading the equipment, intending to station Indian air force units there.[13] New Delhi's plans ran counter to Russia's general line of excluding any foreign military presence in the CIS. Moscow also could have worried that an Indian military presence in Tajikistan would lead Pakistan to extend its interpretation of the concept of "strategic depth" from Afghanistan up to Tajikistan, which would mean the spread of the India-Pakistan rivalry into Central Asia.

Initially Moscow nonetheless seemed more open to an Indian military presence in the region than to a Western presence. In 2005, Sergey Ivanov, Russian defense minister, raised the possibility of Russia and India jointly operating the Ayni base.[14] Ivanov's suggestion seemed to imply that Moscow believed it would be able to control a limited Indian military presence. In

payments for the base, which he in any case preferred to keep. Bakiyev's son Maksim had a large vested interest in continuing the base operations, being deeply involved in the fuel supply business for the base. In 2007, Marat Sultanov, speaker of the Kyrgyz Parliament, extended an offer to Russia to return Russian border guards, withdrawn in 1999, back to the country. China became concerned; it did not want Russian troops on the Kyrgyz-Chinese border. However, the offer was about the southern border of Kyrgyzstan. Bishkek meant to put Russian troops on its border with Uzbekistan. Probably Bakiyev just wanted to offer Russia something it would deny anyway (that is, Russia's desire to not interfere in the complex Kyrgyz-Uzbek relations), but have the ground to say it was not the case that he welcomed only the U.S. military. Russia predictably denied the offer. However, the story indicates that Bakiyev was balancing relations with Russia and the United States. See Евгений Круглов, "Киргизия мечтает о российских пограничниках," *Росбалт*, June 11, 2007, http://www.rosbalt.ru/main/2007/06/11/298860.html.

13. Sudha Ramachandran, "India Air Base Grounded in Tajikistan," *Asia Times*, December 1, 2010, http://www.atimes .com/atimes/South_Asia/LL01Df02.html.

14. "Авиабаза Айни (Гиссар)," *Коммерсантъ*, September 3, 2011, http://www.kommersant.ru/doc/1765768.

subsequent years, though, Moscow moved to oppose any foreign military presence in the CIS, an approach China also favored. In 2008, Russian signed a package of agreements on military cooperation with Tajikistan that provided for Russia's return to the Ayni base without the Indians. The Russian deployment never occurred, however, because the two sides could not agree on the rent price.

China, on the contrary, was always a reliable partner for Russia in resisting "colored revolutions" and foreign military presence; they shared critical views on both issues.[15] China and Russia jointly put into the SCO agenda the issue of U.S. military bases.[16] From 2004, the SCO started requesting that the United States provide a time frame for the withdrawal of its military presence in SCO-member countries. Even those governments who hosted and welcomed a U.S. presence signed onto these relatively soft statements by the SCO, which did not call for immediate U.S. withdrawal. In fact, these SCO statements could be seen as a signal from both Russia and China that the U.S. military presence was tolerated, but closely watched, and would need to be wrapped up at some point.

Frozen Conflicts and War with Georgia

In 2008, when Russia could feel relief from reversing the trend of growing foreign military presence in the CIS, it faced a huge crisis of another sort. After many months of mounting tension and a "war of nerves," in August 2008 Georgia launched a military attack on South Ossetia, a self-declared state existing out of Tbilisi's control since 1993 and maintaining close relations with Russia. In this attack, Russian officers from the ranks of CIS peacekeepers deployed to South Ossetia were killed. The Russian military invaded, moving from South Ossetia to core Georgian territory. Russia then recognized South Ossetia and Abkhazia as independent states, a step it had hesitated to do in the previous 15 years despite many calls from the separatist territories for recognition.

Russia had long been concerned over the problem of the so-called frozen conflicts around the post-Soviet region. These conflicts emerged in the last years of the Soviet Union when various territories rebelled against their parent republics, which were in the process of declaring their sovereignty and independence from Moscow. Armenian-majority Nagorno-Karabakh sought to break away from Azerbaijan, South Ossetia and Abkhazia sought independence from Georgia, and Russian-majority Transnistria moved to separate from Moldova. In some cases, ethnic tensions did not rise to the level of open separatism, but still existed, like in Crimea or southern Kyrgyzstan where Kyrgyz and Uzbek communities clashed in 1990. Following the Soviet collapse, Russia was careful to keep such conflicts from reactivating, as their "unfreezing" could place Moscow in the

---

15. Examples of Chinese views on the issues are discussed in Pan Zhiping, ed., *Central Asia Stricken by "Color Revolution"* (Uriimqi: Xinjiang People's Press, 2006); and Shi Lan, *The First War in 21st Century* (Uriimqi: Xinjiang People's Press, 2003).

16. The alternative view is that "domestic political developments within these hosts (*Uzbekistan, Kyrgyzstan*) initially drove changing attitudes towards the base issue, and then the Central Asian states strategically used or invoked Russia and China to justify these domestically-based decisions." See Alexander Cooley, "U.S. Bases and Democratization in Central Asia," *Orbis* 52, no. 1 (Winter 2008): 65.

uncomfortable position of facing open hostilities with one of the other CIS states, as finally happened with Georgia in 2008.

In the years before 2008, Russia tried to mediate these conflicts. In March 2001, Putin and Eduard Shevardnadze, Georgia's president, reached the so-called Sochi agreements, which were to start the return of Georgian refugees to Abkhazia and to open railway communication between Russia and Georgia via Abkhazia. However, these accords were not implemented. In 2003, Russia offered a plan for resolution for the Transnistria conflict known as the Kozak Memorandum (after Kremlin envoy Dmitry Kozak), promising the reintegration of Transnistria into Moldova with some kind of special political status. The Moldovan government was set to sign the memorandum, but hours before the signing ceremony, President Vladimir Voronin changed his mind after communicating with local representatives of the Organization for the Security and Co-operation in Europe (OSCE) and the U.S. ambassador in Chişinău, who opposed the deal presumably because of concern that giving Transnistria a special political status would give its pro-Russian groups excessive influence over Moldovan politics.

Some expected the conflict with Georgia to have a dramatically negative impact on Russia's influence in the CIS. Yet, while the use of force was not liked by other post-Soviet governments, they all refrained from declarations of solidarity with Mikheil Saakashvili or open criticism of Vladimir Putin, and provided limited political support to Russia.[17]

After the 2008 conflict, Russia started even more actively asserting its influence in the post-Soviet region. Viktor Yanukovych, generally seen as a pro-Russian figure, won the presidential elections in Ukraine in 2010. Opposition to Saakashvili in Georgia grew, impeding his ability to pursue an anti-Russian course.[18] The Georgian opposition then won presidential elections in 2013 and sought to normalize relations with Russia. President Kurmanbek Bakiyev fled Kyrgyzstan after massive street protests in April 2010, and the new Kyrgyz authorities stepped up the pressure over the presence of the U.S. base, which finally closed in 2014. The French military left Tajikistan in 2013. In 2010, Moscow and Dushanbe signed a new agreement on border cooperation, although Tajikistan rejected offers to return Russian border guards to the border with Afghanistan.[19] The German military left Uzbekistan in 2015. And though Tashkent withdrew from the CSTO in 2012, it maintained bilateral military cooperation with Russia.

---

17. The final declaration of the 2008 SCO summit, held shortly after the conflict, had the following item on the issue: "SCO member-states express their deep concern with regard to the recent tension around the South Ossetian question and call upon the respective sides to peacefully resolve existing problems through the path of dialogue. . . . SCO member-states welcome the approval in Moscow on August 12, 2008, of six principles for settlement of the conflict in South Ossetia and support Russia's active role in promoting peace and cooperation in the region." See "Душанбинская декларация," InfoSCO, http://www.infoshos.ru/ru/?id=39.

18. After militarily losing in 2008, Saakashvili started an anti-Russian campaign in Northern Caucasus, primarily on the "Circassians issue," aimed to present Russia as a repressive power in the Northern Caucasus. See Ivlian Haindrava, "A Caucasian Home as Designed by Tbilisi," *Russia in Global Affairs*, no. 2 (2012), http://eng.globalaffairs.ru/number/A-Caucasian-Home-as-Designed-by-Tbilisi-15581.

19. George Gavrilis, *Afghan Narcotrafficking: The State of Afghanistan's Borders* (New York: EastWest Institute, April 2015), 22–23, https://www.eastwest.ngo/sites/default/files/ideas-files/Afghanistan-Borders.pdf

Afghanistan

Throughout the 2000s, Russia did not want NATO's International Security Assistance Force (ISAF) to fail completely in Afghanistan, but it also did not want ISAF to succeed fully.[20] Russia sought to maneuver between these extremes.[21]

From 2009–2010, Afghanistan-related issues rose to the top of Russia's security agenda for the CIS and Central Asia in particular. Russia argued that regional powers should be involved and have more influence on the international efforts to stabilize Afghanistan. At the same time Russia tried to promote CSTO and SCO activity on the Afghan issue. It took Russia a while to have this approach take root in Central Asia.

Russia first pushed for the SCO to take the Afghanistan issue more seriously. In 2009, Russia hosted an international conference on Afghanistan, under the auspices of the SCO, that promoted a more regional approach. In his final remarks at the conference, Aleksey Borodavkin, Russia's deputy minister of foreign affairs, stated: "As I see it, all the presentations at the conference had the idea that the efforts of the international community to stabilize Afghanistan need some rethinking."[22] However, this push for a greater SCO role did not bring much in the way of results over the next several years.

All the Central Asia states except Turkmenistan[23] were concerned about security risks from Afghanistan. Still, for many years they maintained a strong belief in the U.S. commitment to secure Afghanistan, if not for purposes of regional security, then at least for U.S. geopolitical purposes. Like India, they exaggerated Washington's commitment to an enduring geopolitical commitment to Afghanistan, not believing that the United States would focus on developing an exit strategy. Central Asian states were concerned about the potential for the United States to fail though, and hedged these risks primarily by cooperating with their fellow CSTO members.

---

20. Russia's position on "success" was dubious. On the one hand, Russia did not want a complete ISAF success because this would open the way for projects to redirect Central Asia from Russia to South Asia according to the "Greater Central Asia" vision. In 2007, Russia's Ministry of Foreign Affairs (MFA) published the *Review of Foreign Policy of Russian Federation*, which implicitly expressed criticism on the U.S.-backed vision of "Greater Central Asia." On the other hand, Russia doubted ISAF would succeed, as the *Review* explains, "If the Afghan campaign fails and the U.S. and NATO leave Afghanistan, the states of Central Asia and Russia will be left face to face with the consequences of an aggravated Afghan problem, first of all narco-terrorist threats, the rise of fundamentalist sentiments and destabilization of the region." See Министерство иностранных дел, *Обзор внешней политики Российской Федерации* (Moscow: Министерство иностранных дел, 2007), http://archive.mid.ru/brp_4.nsf/0/3647DA97748A106BC32572AB002AC4DD.

21. Ivan Safranchuk, "The Afghan Problem in the Regional Context," *Russia in Global Affairs*, no. 3 (2009), http://eng.globalaffairs.ru/number/n_13594.

22. "Стенограмма заключительного слова заместителя Министра иностранных дел России А.Н. Бородавкина на специальной конференции по Афганистану под эгидой Шанхайской организации сотрудничества, Москва, 27 марта 2009 года," МИД (speech, Moscow, March 27, 2009), http://www.mid.ru/foreign_policy/international_safety/conflicts/-/asset_publisher/xIEMTQ3OvzcA/content/id/300598.

23. Turkmenistan in the late 1990s accommodated itself to the position that it did not face security risks from Afghanistan and could rely prevailingly on economic and diplomatic instruments to deal with it. President Saparmurat Niyazov exercised this approach with Afghanistan, when it was governed by Taliban–al Qaeda coalition and partly by Northern Alliance commanders. President Gurbanguly Berdimuhamedow continued this policy while the ISAF mission was under way.

When the United States started downsizing its military presence in Afghanistan and shifting responsibilities to the Afghan National Security Forces, the Central Asian countries understood that the U.S. exit strategy was real. In turn, they compensated for their delay in apprehending what the United States was doing by exaggerating its scope. Kazakhstan, Tajikistan, and Kyrgyzstan started to rely increasingly on cooperation with the CSTO as their primary line to address Afghanistan-related security challenges. The CSTO intensified its work with member states to be prepared for security risks emanating from Afghanistan.

RUSSIA'S ECONOMIC POLICY IN EURASIA

In the years since Vladimir Putin's ascension to the Kremlin in 2000, Russia pursued two parallel economic approaches in Eurasia. Above all, Russia tried to gather an economic community of post-Soviet countries. The major tool was exploitation of the preexisting economic connections to Russia, especially dependence on Russian energy resources. For many years after the collapse of the Soviet Union, Russia maintained discounted energy prices for all importing CIS states. However, from 2005, Russia started increasing energy prices. Special terms were provided only to those who agreed to join Russian-led integration organizations. Whenever possible, Russia preferred to give loans to countries so they could purchase oil and gas rather than provide direct discounts. Additionally, many CIS producers of both consumer and capital goods depended on access to Russia's expanding consumer market, which was a result of the higher oil prices.

Russia thus intended to gather into an economic grouping those states that needed Russian resources for their industries and households, plus those interested in access to the Russian market for their industries. The countries that fell into this group were Belarus, Ukraine, Moldova, Armenia, Tajikistan and Kyrgyzstan. On purely economic grounds, Georgia should have been included as well, but Tbilisi took such an assertive line in security disputes with Russia that its economic interests became secondary. Uzbekistan did its best to remain outside this group (see below) and tried to pursue an active industrial policy without joining post-Soviet integration projects. Kazakhstan is another special case, maintaining a large number of interconnections with Russia, but not really dependent on Moscow. It therefore played a more independent and its own role in the promotion of post-Soviet integration, in a way figuratively cochairing it along with Russia.

Russia had a different line for those who were big exporters of their own resources and had no or limited interest in guaranteeing their industries access to the Russian market, mainly Azerbaijan and Turkmenistan. Russia got into particularly intensive competition over the volumes and directions of Turkmenistan's gas exports.

Competition over Non-Russian Energy Exports from the CIS

In the 1990s, Russia sought to maximize revenues from energy exports as the primary source of hard currency for its state budget. At the time, energy prices were declining and other energy exporters from the CIS, namely Kazakhstan, Azerbaijan, Turkmenistan, and Uzbekistan, competed with Russia on European and global markets.

Not requiring large volumes of gas and oil from these other producers itself and trying to keep their energy out of the European market, Russia in the 1990s developed a policy of purchasing only small volumes of oil and gas for a low price from its post-Soviet neighbors. This approach was mostly the result of commercial interests, although political considerations related to keeping the other post-Soviet producers from developing direct ties to Europe might have been a factor too.

In particular, Turkmenistan suffered from this approach. Its gas production fell dramatically compared to Soviet times, from around 80 billion cubic meters (bcm) in 1989 to 20–22 bcm in 1999 and a record low 12–13 bcm in 1998. In 1997–1998 transportation of gas from Turkmenistan to Russia was interrupted because Turkmenistan rejected Moscow's terms of low volumes and low prices.

Like Russia itself, other CIS oil and gas exporters badly needed revenues to ease their socioeconomic problems after the collapse of the Soviet Union. Because they experienced problems exporting through Russia, they started looking for alternatives. Diversification of energy export routes surfaced as a major priority for all these countries. Azerbaijan turned to Georgia and Turkey. Kazakhstan started talking to China. Turkmenistan turned to Iran and Pakistan (via Afghanistan). Turkmenistan opened the first pipeline not leading to Russia in 1997, when it began exporting gas to Iran. Kazakhstan's negotiations with China accelerated and Azerbaijan got U.S. and European support for the Baku-Tbilisi-Ceyhan (BTC) oil pipeline across Georgia to Turkey.

With some progress in diversification efforts of CIS energy exporters, but more important, because oil prices went up, Russia changed its attitude in the 2000s, becoming interested in attracting volumes for export from Azerbaijan, Kazakhstan, and Turkmenistan to go through Russian pipelines. This new strategy, however, proved difficult to implement.

Azerbaijan had placed a major stake on the success of the BTC oil pipeline. When it became operational in 2006, Azerbaijan was no longer dependent on Russia for the transit of oil. The opening of the Baku-Tbilisi-Erzurum gas pipeline a few years later did the same for gas. Railway transportation was also available through Georgia. Except for limited volumes, most of Azerbaijan's oil and gas exports henceforth went to Turkish and European markets.

After much effort, Kazakhstan and its American partners in the Caspian Pipeline Consortium (CPC) agreed in 1999 on a pipeline from the Tengiz oil field to the Russian Black Sea port of Novorossiysk. Quickly constructed in 1999–2001, it became operational in late 2001. Russia, however, partly continued to limit volumes. As Kazakhstan's production in the Caspian Sea was growing, Russia for many years sought to delay the CPC pipeline's expansion. Kazakhstan consequently sought to export oil via the BTC pipeline, shipping it by barge across the Caspian Sea to Baku. Meanwhile, Kazakhstan was increasingly cooperating with China, which built oil and gas pipelines from Central Asia in the 2000s and got access to large volumes of Kazakh oil and gas in a very short period of time.[24]

---

24. Estimates vary, but we rely on the estimate that Chinese companies produced 30 percent of the oil and 12 percent of the gas in Kazakhstan on average in 2011. They are present in all regions of Kazakhstan with oil and gas production, plus they have shares in three gas and five oil pipelines. See Константин Сыроежкин, "Китайское присутствие в

A major competition broke out over Turkmenistan. After Ashgabat's first successful diversification effort in opening a gas pipeline to Iran in 1997, other efforts did not progress. A planned Trans-Caspian Gas Pipeline (TCGP) to connect Turkmenistan to the South Caucasus was heavily politicized and lacked a solid technical or commercial background.[25] Besides, this route was hostage to the unresolved juridical status of the Caspian Sea and tensions in Azerbaijan-Turkmenistan bilateral relations. The long-running saga of the proposed Turkmenistan-Afghanistan-Pakistan-India (TAPI) pipeline was always pushed forward by Ashgabat, despite seeming unrealistic to many observers because of obvious security and commercial concerns.

Gazprom needed Turkmenistan's gas to resell to other CIS countries, because cheap Turkmen gas helped to keep Gazprom's prices low. Turkmen gas transported through Russian pipelines was sold to Ukraine, but also to Azerbaijan (before it became a gas exporter itself after 2006), Georgia, Armenia, and Moldova.[26] With world energy prices going up in the 2000s, Gazprom's earnings from such resales within the CIS grew, as Gazprom from 2005 gradually increased prices for CIS importers of gas.[27] Gazprom's approach for exporters, mainly for Turkmenistan, thus evolved from "small volumes for a low price" to "large volumes for a low price." However, Turkmenistan pushed for higher prices. From 2001 to 2006, Russia and Turkmenistan were in very tough negotiations on price, with Ashgabat steadily pushing the prices it demanded from Gazprom up, from $36 per thousand cubic meters (tcm) in 2001 to $100 per tcm in 2006.

Russia increasingly faced competition for Turkmenistan's gas as well. In 2006, Beijing got seriously interested, signing an agreement on construction of a pipeline from Turkmenistan to western China. Following the adoption of a new strategy for relations with Central Asia, the European Union also engaged in negotiations with Turkmenistan on the possibility of Turkmenistan's gas being transported via the Caspian Sea, the South Caucasus, and Turkey to the European market.

From 2007, Gazprom, in response, was willing not only to buy whatever volumes Turkmenistan was ready to produce, but also to pay better prices than Iran or China. It was widely believed by Russian officials that Turkmenistan would not have any gas for other buyers, as Gazprom

---

Казахстане: экспансия или партнерство," *Большая Игра: политика, бизнес, безопасность в Центральной Азии* 24, no. 3 (2012): 6–8, 18–20.

25. Владимир Милов, "Газ Туркменистана: геополитика и бизнес," *Большая Игра: политика, бизнес, безопасность в Центральной Азии*, no. 2 (2007): 7–8.

26. Татьяна Митрова, "Газ Центральной Азии - вчера, сегодня, завтра," *Большая Игра: политика, бизнес, безопасность в Центральной Азии*, no.1 (2007): 6.

27. Initially Gazprom moved to downsize subsidizing for CIS importers of gas because its stocks were legally opened for foreign investors, which made Gazprom more attentive to private shareholders (who together with the major shareholder, the Russian government, actually funded the subsidies). From 2005, oil and gas prices increased during the next several years. In 2007, importing CIS countries paid on average already more than three-quarters of the European price for Russian oil, but still less than half for gas. See Владимир Чернышев, "Россия-СНГ: торговля расширяется, проблемы остаются," *Таможенное обозрение*, no. 2 (2008). Gazprom learned to earn on resales. Between 2007 and 2009, Russia more actively pushed gas prices up to the European level for importing CIS countries. While the latter complained, Russian businesses cheered the effort. For an article on the topic, see the RBC's business Website: "ФК 'УРАЛСИБ': Газпром; намерен добиться экспортных цен для стран СНГ и Балтии повышения на 15–40%," РБК, August 30, 2007, http://quote.rbc.ru/comments/2007/08/30/31613732.html.

contracted everything Turkmenistan made available for export. However, this did not stop Turkmenistan from pursuing additional diversification efforts.[28]

In 2007, Russia made a deal with Turkmenistan, as well as Kazakhstan and Uzbekistan (which transit Turkmen gas to Russia), to enlarge the capacity of old Soviet pipelines in order to leave no available volumes on the Caspian shore of Turkmenistan, which undermined the case for a Trans-Caspian pipeline.[29] The agreement floundered over disagreements about how to fund the project, and Gazprom soon lost interest.

With the collapse of oil prices in the second half of 2008 and the subsequent decline of gas prices, Gazprom once again became interested in sending its own volumes first to the European market. It requested a dramatic decrease in the amount of gas it was purchasing from Turkmenistan, requesting in 2009 only about a quarter of the 43.2 bcm it purchased in 2008. Turkmenistan refused and kept pumping the originally contracted volumes through the first three months of 2009 and demanding full payment from Gazprom (based on the "take or pay" provisions of the contract between Gazprom and Turkmengaz). On April 9, 2009, an explosion took place on the pipeline, leading to a major dispute between Russia and Turkmenistan over responsibility. Repair work took the rest of the year, so Gazprom took, and paid, in 2009 only one-quarter of what it had purchased in 2008.

Although the energy prices recovered in 2010, Gazprom never returned again to its position of buying large volumes of gas from Turkmenistan. In the following years its purchases remained around 10 bcm per year. Turkmenistan progressed with construction of the first pipeline to China and made a new deal with Iran. From 2010, both new pipelines became operational and have since expanded further.

Gazprom remained the only European buyer of Turkmen gas. Gazprom accommodated itself to Ashgabat's new Asian projects, on the ground that the more volumes that went from Turkmenistan to Iran and China (as well as potentially to India and Pakistan should TAPI ever be built), the less would be left for the European market. The EU did not act up to its declarations and de-factor withdrew from active competition. After this Gazprom found acceptable balance with China and Iran. Consequently, with this result the intensive competition over Turkmen's gas calmed down after 2009.

Post-Soviet Economic Integration

As Jeffrey Mankoff rightly pointed out, "In one form or another, reintegrating the states of the former Soviet Union has been on Russia's agenda almost since the moment the Soviet Union collapsed."[30] Back in 1995, Russia, Belarus, and Kazakhstan had first signed an agreement to establish a Customs Union (CU). In 1996, the same three countries plus Kyrgyzstan signed a new treaty

---

28. Иван Сафранчук, "Развитие газовой инфраструктуры в Центральной Азии: газа хватит не всем," *Экономическое обозрение Евразэс* 12, no. 4 (2007): 14–16.

29. For a more in-depth discussion, see И.А. Сафранчук, "Трансформация энергетического рынка Евразии: фактор туркменского газа," in *Россия и АТР: переспективы газового сотрудничества* (Moscow: МГИМО, 2012), 153–158.

30. Jeffrey Mankoff, "Eurasian Integration: The Next Stage," *Central Asia Policy Brief*, no. 13 (December 2013), 1, https://app.box.com/s/39m175znb3155e4eo16a.

on deepening integration in economic and humanitarian spheres. That treaty even set the goal of creating a Common Economic Space (CES), with common markets for goods, services, capital, labor, plus common transport, energy, and information systems. Then, in 1999, these four states plus Tajikistan signed new treaties on CU and CES. On October 10, 2000, the presidents of Belarus, Kazakhstan, Russia, Tajikistan, and Kyrgyzstan signed the agreement to establish the Eurasian Economic Community (EurAsEC), which entered into force in May 2001.

EurAsEC was expected to restart post-Soviet integration, which had stumbled in the 1990s, and to finally implement the CU and CES agreements. The idea seemed appealing. Three more countries joined EurAsEC as observers: Moldova and Ukraine in 2002, and Armenia in 2003. However, as the number of involved states grew, Moscow increasingly needed to take into consideration the views of its EurAsEC partners, which slowed down progress toward integration.

Kazakhstan was not just an active supporter of integration plans, but a contributor to their very emergence. For President Nursultan Nazarbayev, the notion of "competitiveness" had remained a lodestar since the early days of independence. Kazakhstan's population of around 16 million was too large to live off the revenues from natural resources, but the domestic market was also too small to absorb the entire production of Kazakhstan's industry. For other parts of the economy to develop (besides energy and metallurgy industries, which were welcome on global markets), Kazakhstan needed foreign markets and partners. Astana came to believe that post-Soviet integration would encourage diversification and economic growth.

Belarus was extremely dependent on the Russian market and on discounted Russian energy to keep local industries running. Given Moscow's political and economic interest in integration, Aleksandr Lukashenko, president of Belarus, calculated that the more integration he accepted (while preserving Belarus' political sovereignty), the easier it would be to get subsidies from Russia, which was important to run his political system.

Kyrgyzstan and Tajikistan were interested in maintaining their access to discounted Russian energy, plus to Russia's and Kazakhstan's labor markets for their large number of economic migrants. Both also sought Russian investment for major infrastructure projects, first and foremost large hydroelectric power stations. This kept them attentive to Russian and Kazakh positions on integration.

Moldova and Armenia also relied on discounted Russian energy and were interested in keeping close economic ties with Russia. Geopolitical considerations were important as well, as both states tried to balance relations with Russia and the West. And Armenia, at the end of the day, depended on Russia for its security.

For Ukraine, the situation was simple in terms of pure economic realities, but complicated if accounting for geostrategic ambitions. Local oligarchs made fortunes from export-oriented heavy industries, like metallurgy, and on energy-related businesses, both of which depended on discounted Russian oil and gas to remain viable. At the same time smaller Ukrainian businesses exported agricultural and light industrial goods (mostly uncompetitive on other markets) to Russia and the CIS. Ukrainian big and small businesses were thus a beneficiary of economic growth in the CIS in general and in Russia in particular. As sales grew, Kyiv had more and more of a practical interest in integration. Still, its ambition was to have free-trade arrangements with Russia (even better with the whole CIS) and at the same time with the European Union, allowing Ukraine to buy and sell in both directions on presumably preferred terms and act as a bridge between Russia and the European Union.

EurAsEC failed to reconcile all these interests of members and observers and was unable to deliver practical results. Documents multiplied, but neither a CU nor a CES materialized. Tajikistan, Kyrgyzstan, Moldova, and Armenia were comfortable with keeping integration at a rhetorical/theoretical level. Even more important, Ukraine did not want to change its status in EurAsEC from an observer to a full member. This stance excluded deeper integration within EurAsEC, but did not preclude it in some other institutional frameworks.

EurAsEC consequently adopted a multispeed ("multilevel" in Russian terminology) approach to integration. In February 2003, the presidents of Belarus, Kazakhstan, Russia, and Ukraine declared their intention to form a CES among their four states. They worked over the next year on a package of technical documents to establish the CES. In September 2004, the four presidents approved these documents.

The 2004 Ukrainian election, which precipitated the Orange Revolution, ended with the pro-Western Viktor Yushchenko taking power in December.[31] Moscow nevertheless tried to keep Kyiv engaged in negotiations to finalize the CES, with no results. Yushchenko wanted to keep Ukraine's existing free-trade agreements with Russia and the CIS, but not move any further on integration. With regard to the CES, Kyiv agreed only to participate in the Customs Union, but rejected any supranational organs (such as a commission to set tariffs), effectively demanding revision of the prepared CES agreements and blocking the inauguration of the CES.

In 2006, Belarus, Kazakhstan, and Russia agreed to proceed with further integration efforts among themselves. At the same time they took a functional step back. They agreed to work for the time being only on the CU, but not the CES. Tajikistan and Kyrgyzstan announced their interest to join later on. In October 2007, Belarus, Kazakhstan, and Russia signed a formal treaty on the CU and began detailed talks on its practical aspects. In June 2009, most of the documents for establishing the CU were approved, and it became operational beginning on July 1, 2010. Within months, the leaders of Belarus, Kazakhstan, and Russia agreed to move forward on establishing a new edition of the CES beginning in January 2012.

In late 2011, Russia, Kazakhstan, and Belarus agreed to further upgrade their integration by creating a Eurasian Union. Russian president Putin described it as a "qualitatively new level" of integration, "merging of natural resources, financial and human capital" to "make the Eurasian Union competitive" and stand "alongside with other key world actors and regional structures—namely, the EU, the US, China, APEC [Asia-Pacific Economic Cooperation]"[32] while Kazakh president

---

31. Opposition candidate Viktor Yushchenko argued that Ukraine should join the European Union and NATO, while President Leonid Kuchma's preferred successor, Viktor Yanukovych, as prime minister had been one of the founders of the CES.

32. Владимир Путин, "Новый интеграционный проект для Евразии - будущее, которое рождается сегодня," *Известия*, October 3, 2011, http://izvestia.ru/news/502761.

Nazarbayev said the new union "has every chance to become an integral part of the new world architecture."[33]

While Russia, Kazakhstan, and Belarus started the CU in 2010, agreed to the CES in 2011, and then throughout 2012 engaged in negotiations on the Eurasian Union, Ukraine was negotiating an agreement on deepening its economic and political ties with the European Union.

In May 2009, the European Union adopted its Eastern Partnership (EaP). Moscow was suspicious, but initially viewed the program as an instrument of European soft power deployed as part of a competition for influence in the post-Soviet region. However, it soon became obvious that besides its rhetorical aspects, the EaP had important economic underpinnings, aiming to create a Deep and Comprehensive Free Trade Area (DCFTA) with participating countries through the signing of association agreements (AAs). Moscow saw this initiative as a transparent bid to compete with Russian-sponsored integration projects in Eastern Europe and the South Caucasus.

Ukraine, Moldova, and Armenia quickly became interested in the DCFTA. Even Belarus had some interest in the EaP. In late 2009 and early 2010, President Lukashenko slowed down the tempo of negotiations on the CU and toughened his bargaining position. In the spring of 2010, Putin said that the CU would start without Belarus if Minsk continued to need more time for consideration. At that point Belarus quickly turned to the CU. During the same period, the two-year rapprochement (late 2008 until late 2010) between the European Union and Belarus ended. Belarus, not having European sanctions imposed on it during 2009 and 2010, then faced a new wave of sanctions in January 2011 following the suppression of the Belarusian opposition after the presidential elections in November 2010. For many people in the CIS, however, Belarus' decision to join the CU and the heavy wave of EU sanctions that followed did not seem to be absolutely unconnected.

From 2010 through 2014, Russia and the European Union put forth competing offers to Moldova, Armenia, and Ukraine to join either the EaP or the CU. Significant debates broke out in the affected countries, particularly in Ukraine.

The Crisis over Ukraine

Facing infighting with his one-time allies in the Orange Revolution, Ukrainian president Yushchenko became intensely unpopular and chose not to run for reelection in 2010. He was succeeded as president by the loser of the Orange Revolution, Viktor Yanukovych. When he took office in February 2010, Yanukovych's top priority was to get a gas discount from Russia.

A year before, in January 2009, Prime Minister Yulia Tymoshenko had signed a long-term contract with Russia, which committed Ukraine to paying European and oil-linked prices for gas beginning in 2010. The deal was connected in part to Tymoshenko's rivalry with President Yushchenko and some oligarchs close to him, whom she wanted to push out as middlemen in the gas trade. But rising oil prices meant that oil-linked gas prices increased dramatically from the beginning of 2010, exactly the moment when Yanukovych took office.

---

33. Нурсултан Назарбаев, "Евразийский Союз: от идеи к истории будущего," *Известия*, October 25, 2011, http://izvestia.ru/news/504908.

Russia agreed to provide a discount only in exchange for signing a 25-year lease for the Russian Black Sea Fleet at the naval base in Sevastopol (on the Crimean Peninsula). Yanukovych anticipated facing domestic blowback from signing such an agreement and tried to alter the terms just hours before the signing. Finally, because of the need for reduced gas prices to keep the economy running, he agreed to Russia's terms and signed the agreement in Kharkiv on April 21. Almost immediately, Yanukovych faced a blast of criticism (up to an accusation of national treachery) from the opposition, notably Tymoshenko's party.

Despite this Kharkiv agreement, Yanukovych and Prime Minister Mykola (Nikolay) Azarov remained fully committed to getting the AA with Brussels. In late 2011, the AA was ready and awaited final approval. The two sides initialed it in March 2012, and it was ready for signing by the summer. The EU, however, postponed the signing, imposing political conditions that included the freeing of Tymoshenko, who had been arrested on corruption charges in 2011.[34]

Ukraine waited through most of 2012 with the AA ready, but in the autumn it renewed contacts with the CU, signing a memorandum on trade cooperation. This could be seen as Yanukovych attempting to pressure the European Union by demonstrating that the CU is an alternative. Probably Brussels viewed his approaches to the CU in such terms, and preferred to stay firm on its demand for Tymoshenko's release. However, it is also possible that Azarov's cabinet had seriously begun to reconsider the value of the proposed AA, not merely seeking to improve its bargaining position. Azarov made the calculation that Ukraine would need $160 billion over 10 years to modernize local industries to compete successfully with EU producers and take full advantage of the AA.[35]

By early 2013, the Ukrainian position was fully shaped. Kyiv wanted cooperation both with the CU and the European Union. Brussels argued that the DCFTA was not compatible with Ukraine's full membership in the CU. The Europeans agreed that the DCFTA would be compatible with Ukraine-CU cooperation (with Ukraine being an observer in the CU or taking any other status except membership) and Ukraine's participation in the CIS free-trade agreement.[36] During February and March, Prime Minister Azarov told Brussels that Ukraine envisioned exactly some kind of cooperation with the CU falling short of full membership. Azarov and Yanukovych seemed to believe that the European Union would not let Ukraine go fully into the CU, and would provide some special terms to lure it away from Russia. Kyiv similarly concluded that Russia so much wanted to get

---

34. After Yanukovych came to power, Tymoshenko came under pressure as a few criminal investigations were started against her. In August 2011, she was arrested. This was likely due to a combination of many motivations, from personal revenge to the pragmatic plan to sentence her for exceeding authority when she signed the 2009 gas contract with Russia. The latter could theoretically undermine the legality of the contract as such and make Russia more likely to agree to further price reductions. Tymoshenko described her case as political suppression. The European Union predictably supported this argument and demanded that Tymoshenko be freed. Paradoxically, Tymoshenko and the European Union defended not only the innocence of the ex-premier, but also the full legality of the gas contract, which gave Russia strong power over any Ukrainian government bound by it.

35. Николай Азаров, *Украина на перепутье. Записки премьер-министра* (Москва: Вече, 2015).

36. This position was reflected in many statements made by EU officials. See, for example, Štefan Füle, "Statement on the pressure exercised by Russia on countries of the Eastern Partnership" (speech, European Parliament Plenary, Strasbourg, September 11, 2013), http://europa.eu/rapid/press-release_SPEECH-13-687_en.htm.

Ukraine into the CU that Moscow would offer it some special terms. In May 2013, Ukraine signed an agreement with the CU, which allowed Ukraine to engage, without membership, in the work of CU bureaucracies, a step Kyiv probably mistook for the possibility of gaining some special status without joining as a full member.

However, by the end of the summer of 2013, Azarov's government finally realized that the European Union would not agree to Ukraine being a member of the CU and having the AA with the European Union simultaneously. Russia also made clear that Ukraine would not get any special status with the CU and should join as a full member, like all others, and that Ukraine could not simultaneously have CU membership and the EU association agreement.[37] The flow of Ukrainian exports to Russia was then interrupted at the border in July and August 2013. Ukraine finally got the point that it would have to choose.

As noted in April 2013 by Steven Pifer, former U.S. ambassador to Ukraine, "The combination of increasing conditionality from the European Union, a continued hard line from Russia and declining interest from the United States narrows Kyiv's freedom of maneuver," with Ukraine likely "being left in a gray zone of insecurity between Europe and Russia."[38]

Faced with this blunt reality, which Yanukovych was late to recognize, Kyiv urged Brussels and Moscow to meet with it trilaterally to work out a compromise solution. Moscow agreed, but the European Union dismissed the offer.

Yanukovych then decided not to sign the AA at the Vilnius summit of the EaP in late November 2013, although he attended it.[39] EU officials received Yanukovych very coldly and, as if to emphasize the point, met in Vilnius as well with a delegation headed by Vitaly Klitschko, an opposition leader and one of the leaders of the street protests that had broken out in Kyiv in the aftermath of Yanukovych's decision not to sign the AA. Opposition leaders were promising to sign the deal should they take power in Ukraine. With protests continuing to expand in Kyiv after the Vilnius summit, Yanukovych came to believe that the European politicians had written him off.

Yanukovych then had little choice but to pursue talks with Russia for urgent financial assistance. At the same time (taken by observers as "in exchange"), he agreed to negotiate full membership in the CU/CES and, presumably, the Eurasian Union.

What happened next is well known. Expansion of the protests, including attacks on government buildings with gunfire and cocktail bombs, and bloody attacks by police on protesters did take place. Government and protest leaders provided different accounts of these events. In late February 2014, Yanukovych fled into exile in Russia. The postrevolutionary government in Kyiv

---

37. In late summer and through autumn 2013, President Putin and Prime Minister Dmitry Medvedev made a number of such statements. See, for example, "Украина не может быть одновременно и в ЕС, и в Таможенном союзе, подтвердил Путин," ТАСС, October 25, 2013, http://tass.ru/arhiv/711133.

38. Steven Pifer, "External Influences on Ukraine's European Integration," Brookings Institution, April 1, 2013, http://www.brookings.edu/research/articles/2013/04/01-ukraine-european-integration-pifer.

39. At the summit, Yanukovych complained to European politicians that they had pushed him toward a very hard choice, which he ultimately did not want to make, and finally expressed hope that Ukraine would be able to sign the AA at the following year's summit.

proceeded to sign the AA, although implementation of the DCFTA was pushed back until the start of 2016.

In the spring of 2014, local Crimean authorities, with military support from Russia, separated from Ukraine and joined Russia following a referendum. In some other southern and eastern provinces the local population protested against the new authorities in Kyiv, which led to new conflicts. In parts of the Donetsk and Luhansk regions, these conflicts escalated to open separatist rebellion against Kyiv and actual civil war.

The intensity of Russia-EU competition over Ukraine kept the attention of all the other affected countries. Moldova and Georgia signed their respective AAs in Vilnius. Like Ukraine, Armenia refused. Azerbaijan meanwhile had refrained from even engaging in active negotiations on an association agreement.

In May 2014, Putin, Nazarbayev, and Lukashenko signed the treaty to create the Eurasian Economic Union at the start of 2015. In June 2014, Armenia joined the treaty and became a member from December the same year. Kyrgyzstan joined the treaty in December 2014 and became a member from August 2015.

After nearly five years spent on the Eurasian Union, the results for Russia were mixed. Putin had to agree to reduce it to the Eurasian *Economic* Union. He had to extend implementation over a decade, without being certain of Kazakhstan's and Belarus's commitment to the project over such an extended period of time. He faced direct counter-efforts from the European Union and the United States, as well as China's less overt dislike—not to mention the failure to bring Ukraine into the nascent union.

Putin and his team were close to success in Ukraine. Putin's team believes that during 2012 and 2013 they had won an honest nonmilitary competition over Ukraine, and finally lost only because of a coup, jointly carried out by the Ukrainian opposition, the European Union, and the United States in the form of the Euromaidan Revolution. From Putin's comments through 2014 and 2015, it appears he remains a committed believer that Ukraine will eventually "return."[40]

Greater Eurasia and Russia's "Turn to East"

Russia intensified its relations with China in an initiative Moscow labeled as its "Turn to East" (also referred to as the Russian pivot to Asia) in 2014. This pivot, however, did not start in 2014. Russian business interest in Asia and the Pacific had surfaced back in the mid-2000s, when Russian exporters sensed the shift of global demand for commodities to Asia, and became eager to develop new export opportunities. The Russian government supported these interests with new infrastructure projects. Business attention to Asia further intensified during the 2007–2009 global financial crisis. Russia's financial and industrial tycoons, who had been implementing aggressive expansion strategies in the 2000s, mostly through mergers, came into the crisis deeply indebted. They started looking for options in Asian financial markets, which was reasonable because they already

---

40. Putin stated, "Ukraine will get on its own two feet and will develop positively, [and] will together with Russia build its future." See Владимир Путин et al., "Встреча с представителями национальных общественных объединений Крыма," Официальный сайт Президента России (meeting with representatives of the national public associations of Crimea, Yalta, August 17, 2015), http://www.kremlin.ru/events/president/news/50140.

planned to expand exports to Asia. The Russian government also delved further into Asian economic affairs, hosting the 2012 APEC summit in Vladivostok. After the failure of the last try during the 2007–2009 global economic crisis to revive the agenda for deeper cooperation with the European Union, Russia came to see Asia as a new center of gravity for the world economy. Consequently, the importance of the APEC summit was growing for Russia. Russian experts raised their voices in favor of more engagement in Asia.[41]

Russia's pivot focused on China as Moscow's most important partner in Asia. Moscow had aspirations to develop ties with a wider range of Asian states, but, especially after the imposition of Western sanctions in 2014, the role of China became paramount. Sergey Karaganov, a prominent Russian strategist, then suggested the concept of a Greater Eurasia, which implied that Moscow and Beijing should coordinate their approaches to Eurasia in pursuit of shared strategic goals.[42]

Many Russian strategists believe that is possible. Their thinking is based on the assumption that the world is fragmenting into two large groupings: the extended West under U.S. leadership and a Greater Eurasia. Within this Greater Eurasia, Russian strategists argue that China is coming to understand that it cannot stand alone, nor does it have the bandwidth to construct its own regional grouping. Beijing's most realistic alternative, in this telling, is to join an existing regional bloc such as Russia's Greater Eurasia. In practice, this Greater Eurasia can even grow out of the SCO that, including its observers, stretches all the way from the Black and Baltic seas to the Persian Gulf and the Indian, Pacific, and Arctic oceans, and whose constituent states are to varying degrees resistant to social, cultural, and political Westernization.

On this base or another, the Chinese leadership accepted the Russian proposal for cooperation between the Eurasian Economic Union and the Chinese-sponsored Silk Road Economic Belt (SREB). On May 8, 2015, the two countries signed a joint declaration calling for cooperation between the two.

Of course, the success of future cooperation relies on certain assumptions, the most important of which is that China actually views the world in the way Russian specialists think it does. Regardless, for now the idea of Greater Eurasia is being implemented as a key component of Russian foreign policy.

On December 3, 2015, in his address to the Federal Assembly (Russian parliament), President Vladimir Putin proposed that the Eurasian Economic Union, SCO, and Association of Southeast Asian Nations (ASEAN) consult on a new economic partnership. Now Russian authorities speak about a transcontinental partnership of the Eurasian Economic Union, SCO, and ASEAN.

---

41. Alexander Lukin, "Russia to Reinforce the Asian Vector," *Russia in Global Affairs*, no. 2 (2009), http://eng.globalaffairs.ru/number/n_13030.

42. Sergey Karaganov, "A Turn to Asia: The History of the Political Idea," *Russia in Global Affairs*, January 13, 2016, http://eng.globalaffairs.ru/pubcol/A-turn-to-Asia-the-history-of-the-political-idea-17926.

03

Russia in a Reconnecting Eurasia

In historical perspective Russia cherishes its civilizing/Europeanizing role for Central Asia. In the nineteenth century, when Russia took control of Central Asia, Europe viewed the region as distant Asian lands. When the Soviet Union dissolved, conversely, the region was naturally taken to be part of a bigger Europe, able to accept Western values.

In practical terms most of the infrastructure existing in the 1990s went from Central Asia and the South Caucasus through Russia. Russia definitely wanted to earn commercially on its connecting role, which was already far from pushing for isolation of the new independent states.

As described above, Russia was resistant to nearly all diversification projects aimed at giving the South Caucasus and Central Asian states transport/export routes bypassing Russia. Usually this resistance is viewed by Western experts as an indication of Russia's strategic goal of keeping a dominant political position in the region.

However, other interpretations are also possible. Russia could resist diversification projects aimed at bypassing it for mostly commercial—not strategic—considerations. Initially in the 1990s, Russia treated other CIS oil and gas exporters as its competitors during this time of low prices. Over time, with prices increasing, Russia learned to earn income on transiting/reselling other CIS states' hydrocarbons on the European market. Russia thus did not want to lose revenues it had earned as the major connector and transit route. Besides, Russia is always very sensitive to Western intentions to diminish Russia's role in the CIS space.[1] Consequently, Russia saw U.S.-backed diversification projects as a way of undermining its own influence more than facilitating the development of the new independent states.

Russia, from the early 1990s, had always tried to gather an economic community of post-Soviet countries. Within this line Russia was far from keeping its partners isolated from the outside world.

---

1. Even in the times of the Clinton administration the U.S. government injected geopolitical considerations of preventing a Russian-Iranian axis and for this "isolating Iran and diminishing Russia's role in Caspian energy development." See Fiona Hill, "A Not-So-Grand Strategy: U.S. Policy in the Caucasus and Central Asia Since 1991," Brookings Institution, February 2001, http://www.brookings.edu/research/articles/2001/02/foreignpolicy-hill.

On the contrary, Russia, throughout most of the 2000s, pursued this integration under the rubric "together to Europe." This approach allowed Putin in his first two terms as president to reconcile post-Soviet integration with a generally West-friendly foreign policy. Such was the mainstream thinking at the time: Russia and other CIS countries should, together as an economic grouping, fit into a globalizing world economy. In this case, again Russia intended to play a connecting role.

So Russia hardly had strategic reasons for isolating the South Caucasus or Central Asia from the globalizing economy. Still, Russia sought to exploit its connecting role, and resisted diversification of connecting options for South Caucasus and Central Asia that would diminish its own centrality.

European regulators, however, blocked Russian corporate efforts to gain access to European technology through mergers, which had looked financially affordable in the 2007–2009 crisis. Moreover, the European Union declared its own more active policy in Eurasia with the EaP in 2009 for Eastern European and South Caucasus parts of the CIS space and a separate strategy in 2007 for Central Asia. The EU intended to deal with all these regions directly without Russia's connecting/mediating role. These developments left little room for the "together to Europe" model of Russian-led integration. In the aftermath of the 2007–2009 global financial crisis, many in Russia turned to regionalization, with supporters of a regional focus winning out over proponents of globalization.[2] This approach was also shared by some experts in Central Asia.[3]

Russia, Kazakhstan, and Belarus thus turned to building an economic community in Central Asia, the South Caucasus, and Eastern Europe, with the understanding that ideally it should look like the European Union (or the pre–Maastricht Treaty European Community). This meant having weak or no economic borders inside the community, but strong outside borders, aiming to stimulate production and other economic activities within and among member states.

An element of protectionism is inherent within this approach. However, the level of protectionism was under debate inside Russia itself. Calls for economic autarchy were on the rise.[4] This led to more autarchic/isolationistic interpretations of the Eurasian Union while its treaty was under formal negotiations in 2012–2014. However, the official Russian approach was to present regional integration (also referred to as regional consolidation) as a new form of world economic affairs. A

---

2. Леонид Вардомский, "Вопросы Евразийской интеграции," in *Внешнеэкономические связи постсоветских стран в контексте евразийской интеграции*, ed. Л.Б. Вардомский and А.Г. Пылин (Москва: Институт экономики РАН, 2014), 10.

3. See, for example, an Uzbek expert: Рустам Махмудов, "Кризис глобализации и проблемы развития стран Центральной Азии," *Большая Игра: политика, бизнес, безопасность в Центральной Азии* 39, no. 6 (2014): 40–51.

4. While conservatives were the primary drivers for such ideas, over time they went beyond this ideological circle. An interesting example of this is the reference to isolationistic ideas by Mihail Khodorkovsky in 2015 from exile in Switzerland. Interviewed by the famous modern Russian writer Dmitry Bykiv, Khodorkovsky, in responding to the question about what Russia can supply to world markets, said, "We should absolutely not be thinking about this now. The economy of such a large continental country (Russia) can be only autarchic. Now it is important for us to feed ourselves, but not to think about competition with China. Russia is not that much a part of the world, as a world of its own. The main goal of our economy is self-sufficiency." See "Михаил Ходорковский: Путин победит на выборах и уйдет," *Собеседник*, no. 27 (2015), http://sobesednik.ru/dmitriy-bykov/20150723-mihail-hodorkovskiy-putin-pobedit-na-vyborah-i-uydet.

world with regionally integrated, but not isolated, groupings was expected to emerge.[5] The Eurasian Economic Union was supposed to actively participate in international economic affairs as a single united body.

This approach, though far from blunt isolationism, envisioned strengthening of the CU external economic borders, and consequently affected some trade flows in Eurasia. The reexport of Chinese goods had become an integral element of Kyrgyzstan's economy, with many elites arguing that the country should solidify its position as a regional trade hub for Chinese goods.[6] Since the bulk of the goods Kyrgyzstan was reexporting from China went to the markets of other post-Soviet states, this reexport trade was at cross purposes with the logic of the CU and its successors. Once the CU was established and Kazakhstan had hardened its external customs frontier, the reexport business could not continue as before, despite the existence of substantial loopholes.

With Tajikistan the story is similar. If Tajikistan joins the Eurasian Economic Union, it would need to toughen the customs regime on the Tajik-Chinese border. More important, it would require a serious hardening of Tajikistan's border with Afghanistan. Efforts had been made over the previous 10 years to develop trade to the south. Five bridges have been built into Afghanistan across the Panj River, and border crossings for people and goods have been opened. Free economic zones operate in those areas to stimulate trade. Trade takes place not just with Afghanistan itself, but also with Pakistan via Afghanistan, with some elites in Tajikistan promoting the idea of a "turn to the south."[7] Tajikistan's membership in the Eurasian Economic Union, if it happens, is likely to impede these southern connections, although this may also result from further deterioration of the security situation in Afghanistan.

The Greater Eurasian vision, which conceptualized Russia's pivot to Asia, refutes the charge of isolationism often leveled at the Eurasian Economic Union. At the 2016 St. Petersburg International Economic Forum, Putin and high-level officials reasserted their belief in the emergence of a global world based on regional blocs. Russia aims to form one such bloc in Eurasia jointly with China, while intending to remain connected to the global economy, both through Asia and through Europe. The Eurasian Economic Union is needed within this framework for broad economic development and reindustrialization. Russia is probably going to forge some balance of protectionism and connectivity.

5. Э.С. Набиуллина, "Министр Э.С. Набиуллина выступила на конференции 'Приоритеты и перспективы региональной экономической интеграции с участием России на постсоветском пространстве, в Европейском и Азиатско-Тихоокеанском регионе,'" Официальный сайт Минэкономразвития России, November 17, 2011, http://economy.gov.ru/minec/press/news/doc20111117_2.

6. Ivan Safranchuk, "Russian Policy in Central Asia: Strategic Context," *L'Observatoire*, November 2014, http://obsfr.ru/fileadmin/Policy_paper/PP8_EN_Safrantchouk.pdf.

7. К.И. Искандаров, "Роль Афганистана в решении транспортных проблем Таджикистана," *Большая Игра: политика, бизнес, безопасность в Центральной Азии* 32, no. 5 (2013): 21–26.

04

Conclusion

Russia has proved to be committed to remaining the central security actor in the Eurasian CIS space. Russia has suspicions of any foreign, in particular Western, military activity in the post-Soviet region, and has resisted any outside military presence.

Russian officials have increasingly described actions in the post-Soviet region by Western powers, especially the United States, as destabilizing. At first, Moscow saw such destabilization as unintentional, the result of the West's failure to understand the realities on the ground in the region. More recently, President Vladimir Putin has come to see the destabilization of states more or less loyal to Russia in the post-Soviet region as being a deliberate aim of Western policy. In his well-known 2007 speech at the Munich Security Conference, Putin spoke about the destabilizing effects of U.S. military operations (although not in direct reference to CIS), presenting this as side effects of Washington's neglect of the interests of others. The view that the United States and its allies ignored Russian interests, especially in Eurasia, has become widespread in the Russian security and foreign policy apparatus.[1] In the summer of 2014, Putin, conversely, argued that the West was deliberately seeking destabilization and the outbreak of "colored revolutions" across the CIS, and ultimately in Russia itself.[2]

At the same time, Russia believes that it did not seek geopolitical competition, but rather had such competition imposed on it by the West, which refused to recognize the legitimacy of Russian interests in the region. Still, Russia had in the past, and probably does not exclude for the future,

---

1. A random voice of disagreement on that is Yevgeny Bazhanov, the reactor of the Russian Diplomatic Academy, which is subordinated to the MFA. In a 2014 interview, he sarcastically dismissed purposeful destabilization (and the "theory of managed chaos" that is popular in Russia) by the United States, although he did so with the outrageous argument that Americans were too stupid for that. See Евгений Бажанов, "Евгений Бажанов развенчал теорию управляемого хаоса," Вестник Кавказа video, February 28, 2014, 3:06, http://www.vestikavkaza.ru/video/Evgeniy -Bazhanov-razvenchal-teoriyu-upravlyaemogo-khaosa.html.

2. "Заседание Совета Безопасности," Официальный сайт Президента России video, July 22, 2016, 13:10, http://www .kremlin.ru/events/president/news/46305/videos.

security cooperation with others in Eurasia. But Moscow is likely to pursue such cooperation as limited and issue centered, meaning engagement on particular problems on an ad hoc basis.

Russia is not likely to be interested only in the use of the transit potential of its own territory, or that of Central Asia, to connect China, Europe, and the Middle East. Russia's strategic interests are wider.[3] Eurasian transit is unlikely to emerge in Russia as a sort of strategic enterprise. For itself and the Eurasian Economic Union, Russia envisions more of a development perspective, one which does not exclude transit, but is not transit centered.

Russian economic ambitions in Eurasia evolved from the simple idea of being a bridge between Europe and Asia to forming a regional, economically integrated grouping, which could be an important player in world economic affairs. After years of developing this vision, Russia did not adopt an isolationist approach to this bloc, but, on the contrary, now sees it as connected to Asian and European economic activities. Still, some elements of protectionism for the Eurasian Economic Union are likely to survive, with the aim of stimulating regional industrial development. Russia will have to reconcile this protectionism for itself and its allies with their mutual interest in expanding connectivity to the global economy.

---

3. In 2006, Vladimir Sorokin, a prominent liberal Russian writer who is considered a living classic, published his anti-utopia *Day of the Oprichnik*. An English version was published in 2012. It features Russia in 2025 with internal degradation, but surviving on fees collected from a big roadway between a progressing China and Europe. This probably illustrates the critical common thinking in Russia on a transit-centered future.

About the Author

Ivan Safranchuk graduated in 1998 from the Moscow State Institute of International Relations (MGIMO) and in 2003 received the degree of candidate of sciences (the Russian equivalent of a PhD) from the Academy of Military Sciences, where his work focused on post–Cold War nuclear strategy. From 1997 to 2001, he worked at the PIR Center for Policy Studies, including as director of the Nuclear Arms Control Project. In July 2001, he opened CDI Moscow, a Russia-based branch of the U.S.-based Center for Defense Information; it was renamed the World Security Institute (WSI) in 2006. Since 2008, Dr. Safranchuk has served as an adviser to WSI while focusing on his private consulting work.

Since 2007, Dr. Safranchuk has published a magazine entitled *Great Game: Politics, Business, Security in Central Asia*. Since 2003, he has been associate professor at MGIMO in Moscow. From 2011 to 2014, he served as deputy director of the Institute of Contemporary International Studies at the Diplomatic Academy of the Russian Ministry of Foreign Affairs. He has been a member of the Advisory Council to the Center on Global Counterterrorism Cooperation since 2011; a member of the Council on Foreign and Defence Policy (SVOP), a community of leading Russian security experts, since 2012; and an adviser to the president of the Diplomatic Academy of Kyrgyzstan since 2015.

Over the past eight years, Dr. Safranchuk has been involved in many projects related to Central Asia and Afghanistan. These include research projects for Russian, U.S., and European organizations and also for international organizations, including the United Nations. He has authored publications on nuclear strategy and arms control, nonproliferation, Central Asia, and Afghanistan.